THE
PROMISE
OF LIFE

"When children (and their parents!) read Bible story books, every turn of the page brings up significant questions. Questions about the most basic ideas— life and death and God's Law—require careful explanations from Scripture. *The Promise of Life* is a brilliant guide to help you and your kids wade into the deep waters of those crucial topics. Atkinson's prose is catchy and faithful, and Marsee's artwork will make you stop and think."

— Gloria Furman, author of *Missional Motherhood*

THE PROMISE OF LIFE

A Big Story about God's Law

JONNY ATKINSON

ILLUSTRATED BY TIMMY MARSEE

GOSPEL GROWN

Louisville, Kentucky

The Promise of Life: A Big Story about God's Law

Copyright © 2019 by Jonathan Atkinson
Illustrations copyright © 2019 by Timmy Marsee

Published by
Gospel Grown
Louisville, KY
www.gospelgrown.org

Hardcover ISBN: 978-1-7336615-4-6
Paperback ISBN: 978-1-7336615-6-0

Scripture quotations are from the ESV® Bible (The Holy Bible, English Standard Version®), copyright © 2001 by Crossway, a publishing ministry of Good News Publishers. Used by permission. All rights reserved.

Printed in the PRC

Jonny Atkinson:

For Owen,
may Jesus give you the gift of blessed life with God.

Timmy Marsee:

For Vera and Violet,
who I pray will receive the promise of life.

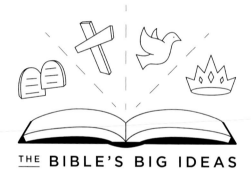

THE BIBLE'S BIG IDEAS

SERIES INTRODUCTION

Children love a good story. They are captivated as they are transported to other times and worlds, meet fascinating characters, hear new phrases, and experience new customs. They are gripped with plots of good versus evil as their innate sense of justice gets roused. And when the story is over, it often lives on with them, as they imagine themselves living in such a world, pretend to be such a character, and utilize their new vocabulary.

The Bible is the greatest story ever told, itself chocked full of extraordinary places and exciting peoples, unique characters and strange customs, new words and novel phrases, memorable events and momentous battles. And all this is within an overarching plot, the greatest triumph of good over evil.

The central message of the Bible is the Gospel, the Good News about Jesus Christ. However, the Bible is a Story made up of many stories, each with their own setting, characters, and plot. These "stories"—if you will—highlight, develop, and illumine various aspects of the Gospel. Therefore, knowing the parts well will deepen our understanding of the whole.

The Bible's Big Ideas is a series for children that focuses on these parts. Each book published within The Bible's Big Ideas highlights an important biblical theme, teaching, or word and traces its development throughout the biblical storyline showing its contribution to the Gospel message. The goal of this series is to help children see how the big picture is made up of many pieces and so deepen their understanding and love of the Gospel.

May the Gospel, the greatest Story ever told, live on with our children as they enter in and embrace this world of the Bible—not simply in their imagination but truly, as the only way to make sense of their story.

TABLE OF CONTENTS

AND THE LORD GOD COMMANDED THE MAN, SAYING, "YOU MAY SURELY EAT OF EVERY TREE OF THE GARDEN, BUT OF THE TREE OF THE KNOWLEDGE OF GOOD AND EVIL YOU SHALL NOT EAT, FOR IN THE DAY THAT YOU EAT OF IT YOU SHALL SURELY DIE."

GENESIS 2:16-17

PART ONE: LIFE WITH GOD

In the beginning, Adam and Eve had LIFE—and not just any LIFE but blessed LIFE with God.

They lived with God in the Garden of Eden, a place that was full of LIFE.

In this Garden stood The Tree of Life. Anyone who ate the fruit from this tree would have LIFE forever.

There was also another tree in the Garden called The Tree of the Knowledge of Good and Evil. God gave Adam a law saying, "Do not eat from The Tree of the Knowledge of Good and Evil or you will die."

This law promised LIFE.

If Adam and Eve obeyed this law, they would be blessed and have LIFE with God in the Garden.

But, if they disobeyed this law, they would be cursed and would die away from God outside the Garden.

One day Satan crept into the Garden as a snake and lied to Adam and Eve. He told Eve, "You will not die if you eat from the Tree of the Knowledge of Good and Evil."

6

Satan was telling Adam and Eve that they could disobey God and still enjoy LIFE with God.

Adam and Eve foolishly believed the Snake's lie and ate the fruit from the Tree of the Knowledge of Good and Evil.

Because Adam and Eve disobeyed God's law that promised them LIFE, they were cursed and punished with death outside the Garden, away from the Tree of Life, and away from God.

God's law promised LIFE, but because Adam disobeyed, it brought death.

...AND IN YOU ALL THE FAMILIES OF THE EARTH SHALL BE BLESSED.

GENESIS 12:3

YOU SHALL THEREFORE KEEP MY STATUTES AND MY RULES; IF A PERSON DOES THEM, HE SHALL LIVE BY THEM: I AM THE LORD.

LEVITICUS 18:5

I WILL MAKE MY DWELLING AMONG YOU, AND MY SOUL SHALL NOT ABHOR YOU. AND I WILL WALK AMONG YOU AND WILL BE YOUR GOD, AND YOU SHALL BE MY PEOPLE.

LEVITICUS 26:11-12

Part Two: The Promise of Life

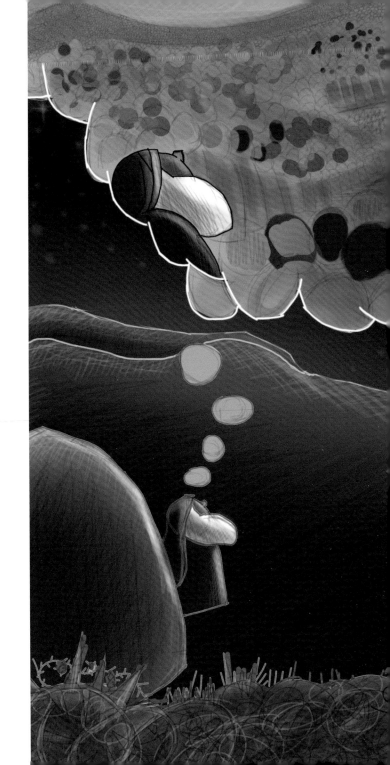

A long time later, God made a great promise to a man named Abraham. He promised to defeat the curse and bring blessing again.

God promised to bless Abraham and make his family into a great people.

God promised to give this great people a new land to live in, a place that was full of LIFE.

God also promised that someone from Abraham's great family would bless all peoples and take away their curse.

Adam's disobedience brought death into the world, but now God was promising to bring LIFE to the world again through Abraham's family.

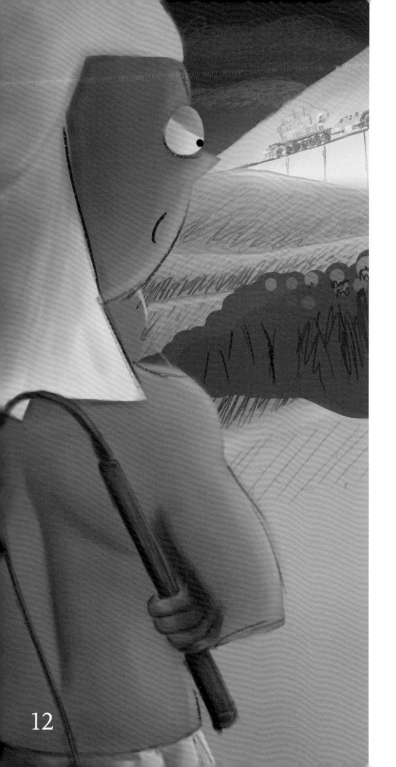

God kept His great promise to Abraham, and his family grew and grew into a great people named Israel.

But before Israel was given LIFE in their new land, they became slaves in a different land called Egypt.

The Egyptians treated the Israelites very badly and even killed many of them.

Israel needed to be rescued from their slavery and death before they could have LIFE in their new land.

And so, Israel cried out to God to set them free.

God heard Israel's cry, and He remembered His great promise to Abraham to give his family a new land to live in, a place that was full of LIFE.

God raised up Moses to be Israel's leader to rescue them from Egypt.

Moses led Israel out of slavery, through the Red Sea, and towards LIFE in their new land.

On the way to their new land, Israel stopped and camped around a big mountain called Sinai.

At Mount Sinai, God came down and spoke with Moses and gave him The Book of Law.

15

In The Book of Law,
God promised that,
if Israel obeyed these
laws, it would go well
for them:

They would have long
LIFE in their new land,
and they would be
blessed,
even the land itself
would be full of LIFE.

But God also promised
that, if Israel disobeyed
His laws, it would not go
well for them:

They would not live long
in their new land,
and they would be
cursed,
even the land itself would
be full of death.

These laws promised
LIFE to Israel in their
new land.

17

And best of all, God promised that, if Israel obeyed His laws, He would come and live with them!

18

These laws promised LIFE—and
not just any LIFE but blessed
LIFE with God!

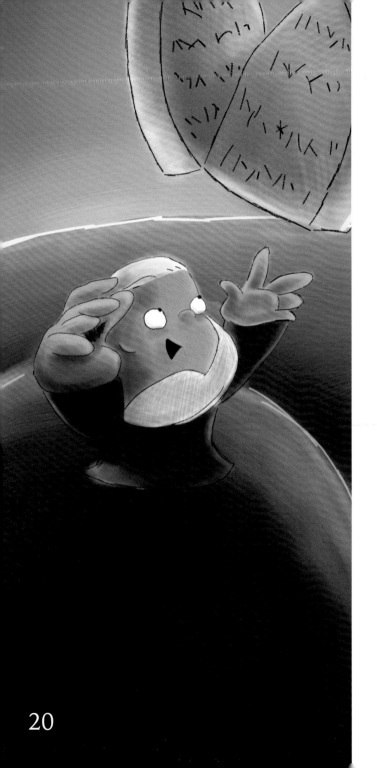

Israel did not have to climb up into heaven or travel far away to find God's Law. Instead, God came down and gave Israel His Law that promised them LIFE.

And these laws that promised LIFE were not hard to obey.

It is not *hard* to leave some of
your harvest for those who
are hungry.

It is not *hard* to leave some
olives hanging on your tree for
the poor to eat.

It is not *hard* to share your
money with others.

These laws that promised LIFE were also good laws.

It is a good thing to give a man back his coat at the end of the day so that he can stay warm.

It is a good thing to be fair and not cheat people in the marketplace.

It is a good thing to bring someone's wandering ox back to them.

God's laws that promised LIFE were not far away, they were not hard laws, and they were good laws.

Jesus answered them, "Truly, truly, I say to you, everyone who practices sin is a slave to sin.

JOHN 8:34

...For apart from the law, sin lies dead. I was once alive apart from the law, but when the commandment came, sin came alive and I died. The very commandment that promised life proved to be death to me. For sin, seizing an opportunity through the commandment, deceived me and through it killed me.

ROMANS 7:8-11

PART THREE: THE LOSS OF LIFE

After Moses had read The Book of Law to Israel, all Israel agreed to obey all of God's laws.

So Moses went back up the mountain to talk with God again.

But while Moses was on the mountain, Israel quickly forgot about God's good laws. They built for themselves an idol, a golden calf, and began worshiping it. They even said that it was the god that had just led them out of Egypt!

Moses had just taught Israel all of God's laws including the law which says, "Do not make idols," and Israel had just agreed to obey them all!

These were easy laws and good laws.
These were laws that promised LIFE
to Israel!

Why did Israel disobey these laws?

27

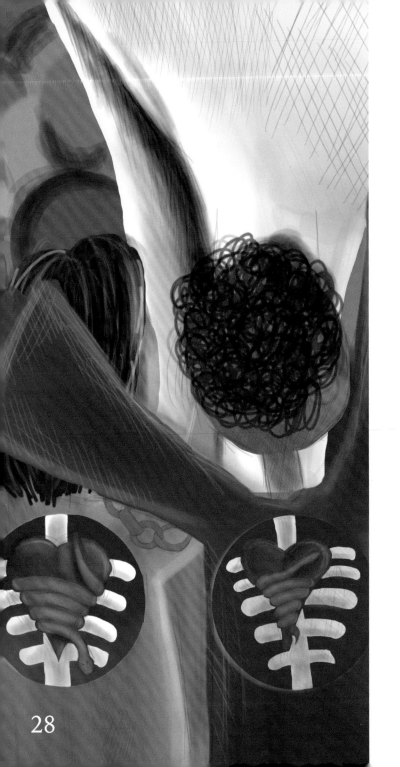

Israel had a serious problem. Even though they were no longer slaves in Egypt, they were still slaves to another master. They were slaves to Sin!

And just like Egypt, Sin would kill Israel.

When Israel heard God's laws that promised LIFE, Sin came alive inside of them and lied to them.

God's Law said, "Do not make idols." But Sin lied and said, "You will not die if you make idols."

Because they were slaves to Sin, Israel foolishly believed the lie and made an idol.

Because they were slaves to Sin, Israel disobeyed God's Law that promised LIFE.

Israel had been set free from slavery in Egypt, but they still needed to be set free from their slavery to Sin before they could have LIFE.

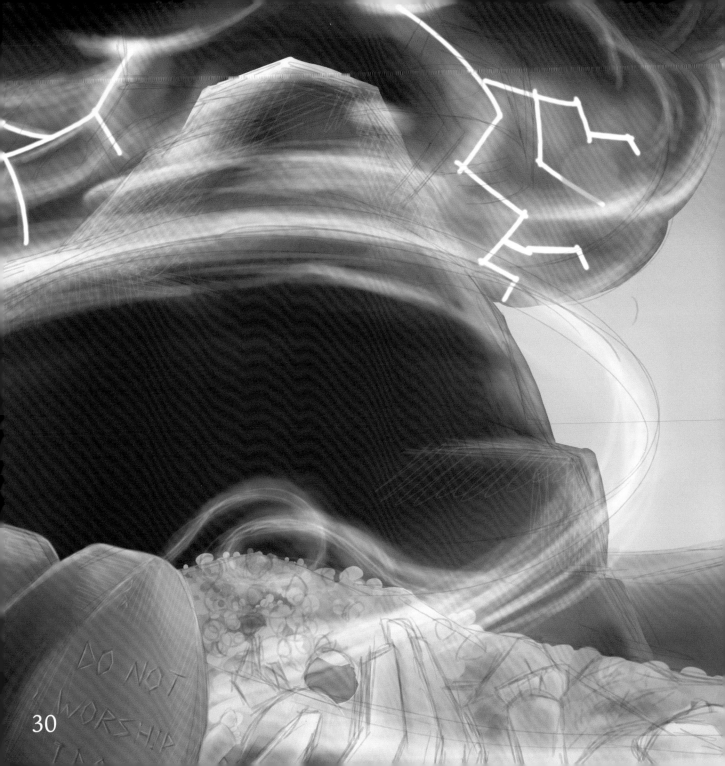

30

Because Israel disobeyed God's Law that promised LIFE, they were punished with death. God sent a destroying plague to Israel, and thousands of them died.

God's Law promised LIFE but, because of Sin, brought death.

31

Even though Israel had disobeyed God's Law, God kept His great promise to Abraham and brought Israel into their new land, a place full of LIFE.

In this new land, God even lived with Israel at the Temple.

However, in this new land, Israel was still a slave—a slave to Sin. So, Israel kept disobeying God's Law for many years.

Because they kept disobeying God's Law, Israel and her land were cursed with death instead of being blessed with LIFE.

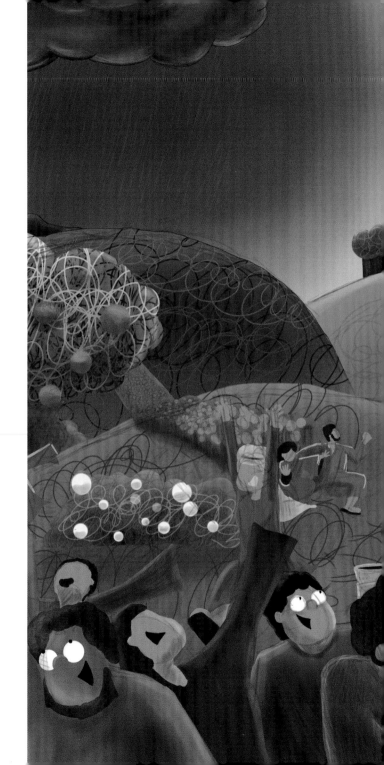

God was patient and slow to anger with Israel. He disciplined Israel and called them to come back to Him, to obey His laws and have LIFE.

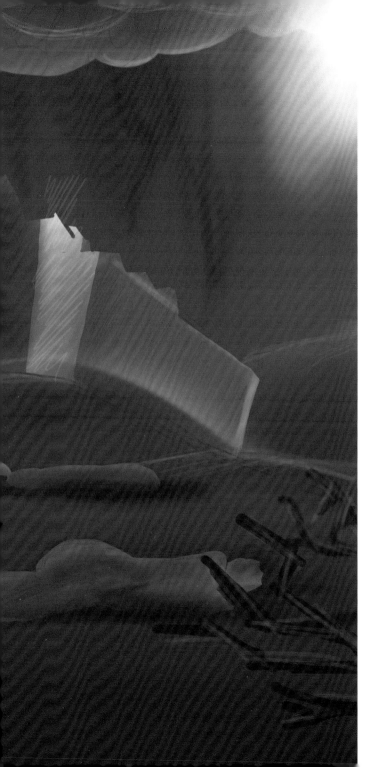

But God's patience with disobedient Israel finally came to an end.

Because they kept disobeying His Law, God brought the worst curse of the Law upon Israel. Israel was punished with death outside their land and away from God.

God left His temple, and it was destroyed. Enemies came and captured Israel's land. Many Israelites were killed, and others were taken away as slaves.

God's Law promised LIFE with God but, because of Sin, brought death away from God.

35

MOREOVER, I GAVE THEM STATUTES THAT WERE NOT GOOD
AND RULES BY WHICH THEY COULD NOT HAVE LIFE

EZEKIEL 20:25

NOW WE KNOW THAT WHATEVER THE LAW SAYS IT SPEAKS TO
THOSE WHO ARE UNDER THE LAW, SO THAT EVERY MOUTH
MAY BE STOPPED, AND THE WHOLE WORLD MAY BE HELD
ACCOUNTABLE TO GOD.

ROMANS 3:19

FOR THE LIFE OF THE FLESH IS IN THE BLOOD, AND I HAVE
GIVEN IT FOR YOU ON THE ALTAR TO MAKE ATONEMENT FOR
YOUR SOULS, FOR IT IS THE BLOOD THAT MAKES ATONEMENT
BY THE LIFE.

LEVITICUS 17:11

Part Four: The Witness to Life

God knew that the Israelites were slaves to Sin. He knew that they would not be able to obey His Law to find LIFE. So why did God give Israel His Law?

God gave Israel His Law to teach them that they were slaves to Sin. God wanted Israel to cry out to Him to be set free from their slavery just like they did in Egypt.

But Israel is not the only one with this serious problem!

God's Law shows that every person in the world is a slave to Sin and under the curse of the Law.

All people need to cry out to God to set them free from their slavery to Sin.

God's Law promised LIFE, but no-one will find LIFE by obeying God's laws.

LIFE with God must come in some other way.

39

God's Law actually taught about this other way, the only way, to have blessed LIFE with God.

God's Law taught that people receive God's blessing for trusting God's great promises.

God's Law taught that those who repent from sin and turn to God would be set free from their slavery to Sin.

God's Law taught that those who confess their sins to God would be forgiven and healed.

God's Law taught that someone else must die to take away the curse of the Law so that others might live.

God's Law taught that someone else must die far
away from God for others to have LIFE with God.

God had made a great promise to Abraham, to bless him and make him into a great people living in a land that was full of LIFE. God had also promised that He would bless the world through Abraham's family. But Abraham's family, Israel, had disobeyed God and did not bring God's blessing to the world. Had God forgotten His great promise?

No! God always keeps His promises.

After Israel had lost LIFE with God in their land, God promised that He was going to do something new and something better.

God's new and better promise was that one day He would set His people free—not from slavery to Egypt, but from their slavery to Sin.

God's new and better promise was that one day He would write His Law—not on stone tablets, but on His people's hearts.

45

God's new and better promise was that one day, He would live with His people—not in a temple, but He would walk among them.

God's new and better promise was that one day, He would take away the curse of the Law so people would have LIFE forever.

This great promise was not just for Israel. Just as God had said to Abraham long ago, He promised that this blessing would come to all peoples in the world, and this blessing would come through someone in Abraham's family.

CHRIST REDEEMED US FROM THE CURSE OF THE LAW BY
BECOMING A CURSE FOR US—FOR IT IS WRITTEN, "CURSED IS
EVERYONE WHO IS HANGED ON A TREE."

GALATIANS 3:13

THROUGH THIS MAN FORGIVENESS OF SINS IS PROCLAIMED
TO YOU, AND BY HIM EVERYONE WHO BELIEVES IS FREED
FROM EVERYTHING FROM WHICH YOU COULD NOT BE FREED
BY THE LAW OF MOSES.

ACTS 13:38–39

Part Five: The Gift of Life

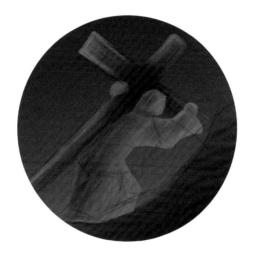

A long time later, Jesus was born into Abraham's family.

Jesus perfectly obeyed all of God's laws. He never once disobeyed God.

Adam disobeyed and Israel disobeyed, but Jesus always did what pleased God.

Jesus was the One from Abraham's family who brought God's blessing to all peoples.

Because of Sin, God's Law brought death to the world, but God brought LIFE to the world through Jesus.

Every person in the world has disobeyed God's Law, and every person is under the curse of the Law deserving to die away from God.

But God sent Jesus to save His people from the curse of the Law.

To do this, Jesus had to make the most dreadful and incredible swap ever.

Jesus gave his perfect life of always obeying God in exchange for His people's life of disobeying God.

Jesus gave His people God's blessing, and He took the curse of the Law from them.

Under the curse of the Law, Jesus died away from God so His people could have LIFE with God.

Every person in the world is born a slave to Sin.

But, when Jesus died on the cross, He destroyed Satan and the power of Sin.

Now, all those who trust in Jesus mysteriously die with Him and are set free from the power of Sin.

Now His people are set free to serve God and not Sin.

After Jesus died, He was buried in a tomb.

Three days later Jesus was raised back to LIFE and came out of the tomb! Death could not hold Him.

Now, all those who trust in Jesus are mysteriously raised to LIFE with Him and will never die!

Jesus gives the gift of eternal LIFE to all who trust in Him.

Now before faith came, we were held captive under the law...But now that faith has come, we are no longer under a guardian

Galatians 3:23—25

PART SIX: THE CHRISTIAN LIFE

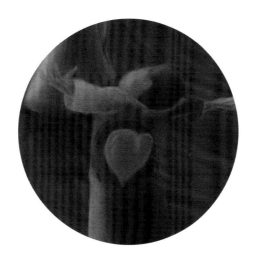

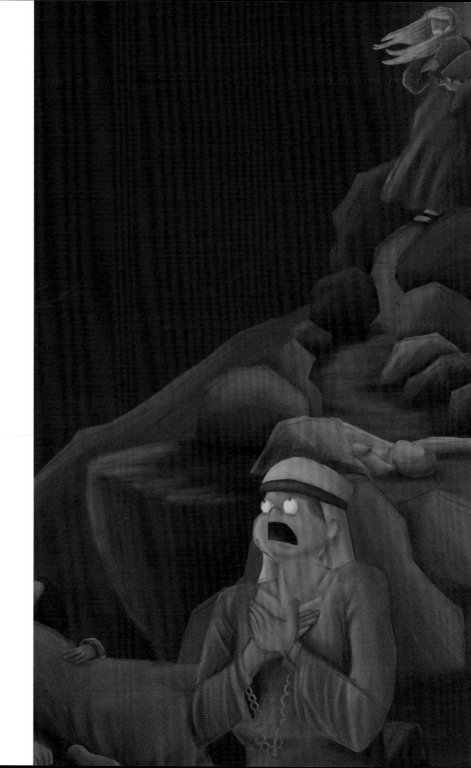

In the old way, God's people were guarded by the Law.

During that time, God's Law brought death because of Sin.

But Jesus has brought the new and better way. God's people now live by faith and no longer need the Law to guard them.

Now, Jesus brings LIFE to all those who trust Him.

The old way has come to an end, but the new and better way lasts forever.

65

In the old way, God wrote The Book of Law on stone tablets for Israel.

But in the new and better way, God writes His Law of Love on His people's hearts.

In the old way, God taught Israel from the Law to love God and love others. Yet, not all Israel obeyed because many of them had evil hearts.

But in the new way, God teaches His people from their heart to love God and love others. Now, all God's people are able to obey because they have new hearts.

However, Satan still lies to God's people.

Sometimes God's people even listen to Satan's lies and disobey the Law of Love.

When they disobey, God's people know that they have done wrong and are sad. God is also sad.

But, because Jesus took away the curse of the Law, God's people will never be separated from God as a punishment. When they confess their sin, God is faithful to forgive them.

God's people are also no longer slaves to Sin.

With God's help, they can now say "No!" to the lies of Satan.

With God's help, they can kill Sin and stop doing the bad things they used to do.

With God's help, they can grow to love other people more and more.

71

Adam and Eve lost LIFE with God in the Garden. But Jesus gives LIFE with God as a free gift to all who trust Him.

However, in this world, God's people do not live in a land with God.

God's people live all over this world, not in one special place with God.

But Jesus is preparing a new world for His people to live together with God.

God's people are waiting until Jesus comes back to bring
them home to this new world, a place full of LIFE.

To the one who conquers I will grant to eat of the tree of life, which is in the paradise of God.

REVELATION 2:7

Behold, the dwelling place of God is with man. He will dwell with them, and they will be his people, and God himself will be with them as their God. He will wipe away every tear from their eyes, and death shall be no more, neither shall there be mourning, nor crying, nor pain anymore, for the former things have passed away.

REVELATION 21:3-4

PART SEVEN: THE FUTURE LIFE

All people who keep trusting Jesus until the end will come to live in the new world, a place that is full of LIFE.

All their names are written in the Lamb's book of LIFE.

They will be given a crown of LIFE.

They will drink from the river of the water of LIFE.

They will finally come and eat from The Tree of Life.

And death will be gone forever.

And best of all, all those who trust in Jesus will have LIFE forever—and not just any LIFE, but blessed LIFE with God!

81

...LET THE ONE WHO IS THIRSTY COME; LET THE ONE WHO
DESIRES TAKE THE WATER OF LIFE WITHOUT PRICE.

REVELATION 22:17

PART EIGHT: YOUR LIFE

Everyone is born a slave to Sin, even you. You have disobeyed God's Law and are under its curse. You deserve the punishment of death away from God.

But God sent Jesus into the world to set people free from their slavery to Sin. God sent Jesus into the world to take away the curse of the Law and bring blessing. God sent Jesus into the world so He could give people the free gift of LIFE.

You need Jesus to set you free from Sin, take away your curse, and give you the free gift of eternal LIFE.

You cannot get LIFE by obeying God's laws.
But, if you trust in Jesus, He will give you the gift of LIFE with God.

Have you trusted in Jesus to take away your curse and give you the gift of LIFE?

Have you been set free from Sin to love God and love others?

SCRIPTURE INDEX

Note to Parents and Caregivers

The Bible teaches that all people are born slaves to Sin. This becomes apparent early in children when they choose to rebel and disobey the good and easy instructions given to them.

Israel was also given good and easy laws from God. However, due to their slavery to Sin, they lacked the ability to obey God's laws. Furthermore, God's laws actually stirred up Sin inside of them, leading them to disobey even more. Though God's laws really did promise life to all who would obey, they could never give life because of the reality and power of Sin. And so, God's Law only brought death. God therefore had to do for His people what laws could never do: defeat the power of Sin and set His people free by taking their curse, dying on their behalf, and giving His righteousness to them. In other words, the Law promised life, but God gives the free gift of life apart from the Law.

The story of God's Law is a story that reveals everyone's slavery to Sin and also an amazing story of God's grace by which He did for His people that which the law could never do—give life.

Giving disobedient children more and more rules will not set them free from their slavery to Sin. Laws, because of Sin, only lead to death. While rules are good and need to be given, and while we must show our children that their disobedience to rules leads to punishment and ultimately death, we must go further. We must teach them that the reason they disobey good rules is because they are slaves to

Sin, and so they can never earn life with God by obeying rules or trying to be a "good" kid. We must teach them that the most important thing they need is to be set free from the Sin within them and the curse of the Law. Only then can we joyfully give them hope and tell them about Jesus who came to defeat Sin. For all who trust in Jesus to save them, He will set them free from Sin, take away their punishment, and give them the free gift of life with God forever.

It is our hope that this book can be used by the Holy Spirit to expose slavery to Sin in the hearts of children that they may look to the Savior and receive His free gift of life.

Note: Each illustration was drawn with many Scriptures in mind. Look up and read aloud the related verses for each illustration using the Scripture index to see if you and your child can find any corresponding images in the illustration.